Anthology *in* BLUE

Written By:
David Ben Foster

Copyright© 2017 by David Ben Foster

All rights reserved under International and Pan-American copyright conventions. No part of this book may be reproduced, stored in a retrieval system or transmitted in any form, electronic, mechanical, or by other means, without permission of the author or publisher.

Library of Congress Control Number: 2017944982

ISBN: 978-0-9893583-9-2

Manufactured in the United States of America by

Blossom Marketing & Publishing, LLC
Post Office Box 1793
Medina, Ohio 44256-1793

Other works by David Ben Foster

NOVEL
The Ultimate Humanist

POETRY
A View of Ourselves
Meter, Muse & Rhyme
An Epic of Job, the Warrior-Priest - Nominated for 2017 Pulitzer Prize

SHORT STORIES
In Our Town
Market Street

AUTOBIOGRAPHY
Cute as a Button

BIOGRAPHY
Sweat & Blood, A Diary of a Civil War Soldier

In loving memory of my younger
sisters, Peggy Louise LeFever, Loraine Gail Baryak,
Nancy Jane Fisher, and younger brothers, Stanley Howard Foster,
Harold Daniel Foster and Wayne Thomas Foster.

Contents

An Entreaty	3
Answers	8
Anthrópos	9
Betrayal	11
Birthmark	64
Blue Air	5
Camille	12
Can't Write	13
Changeable	14
Contemplations	61
Dante's Glutton	16
Deceptions	36
Desperate	1
Distant	6
Embitter-ness	18
Façade	2
Faded Flowers	19
Fated	20
Ghost of a Chance	22
Happy that you met me…	74
Healed	23
I Am a Ghost	24
Impasse	65
Incomplete	21
Inevitably	68
Intention	59
Interludes	77
Island Adjustment	75
Last Cigarette	60
Last Words	72
Learned to Surrender	29

Less of Me	67
Let Me Be Brave	34
Me?	31
Medication	51
Miasma	56
Mirage	57
Mistress	58
Miscommunication	38
NAM 1968	53
New Year's Eve	46
Not Mine	44
Nothing New	39
Oneness	69
Performing	32
Perception	35
Petty Kings	30
Pitch Blue	54
Platonic Love	70
Quiet Times	4
Regret	48
Repetition	43
Retreat	7
Severe	42
Star-crossed	55
The Black Is Back	52
Then, You	47
The Sense of It	63
Tilted	49
Traveler	50
Wedged	66
What?	41
When, I	45
Wide Nights	62
Wild Flower	78

Desperate

I sell possessions like a junky

hoping for one more financial fix, a fix

that eludes like early morning ocean mist that wisps

away and leaves skin salty, sticky—as I scratch.

Another week of futility

as canker sore spots pinch inner lips

as their slow crawl cause a sour angst.

I'd sell more, but ancestors haunt my sleep

so do rejections—love in particular,

as Zoloft lies to my brain, blaming alcohol.

Tomorrow will repeat disaster, for assets

have been depleted, except for the books in

clutter—my office.

Amazon assists sales;

rejections are kinder;

and summer has warmed the air.

David Ben Foster

Façade

Chained by love, another lonely man

unlike the lucky pair in Key Largo, or

in the Gable-Monroe flick, for

dark is the love that bitterness unmatched, and

too soon un-done;

scuffing beneath the unpleasant veneer of two

lovers who wonder what others think, knowing what they know.

Stress is love gone wrong, a self-affliction,

the cause of pretending.

Why gnaw like animals—anger and fear,

neither from gin nor from a dirty syringe;

darkness has its own life—we are the enigma

that mocks innocents, never appeased.

Un-claw, unfurl your wings;

release yourself from me.

An Entreaty

May the night

draw my last breath

while eternal sirens

usher me away.

I, the ever-erring ass

insensitive, insidious,

the fault of woe;

Alone.

I implore the Holy One

to darken this flickering lamp

bringing light

death alone reveals.

David Ben Foster

Quiet Times

Moments that flash by
like a strobe light's glaring;
stressful thoughts linger
into a senseless state:
her face—my loss
her face—my loss
passion—gone
romance—gone.
our music—died
our music—died.

Blue Air

Sweet perceptions of you
while drinking dirty coffee;
embarrassed at myself
for that scene, that
causes me to sit in this stained air.
Looking at two pictures of you
going through a list of what-ifs
wondering… tired… with a headache.

David Ben Foster

Distant

You're music—no beat;
winter wind, in south Florida;
proof that there is a born loser;
an ingrown hair, on a bald head;
missing tooth in a crooked smile;
a welcome sight on a witch hunt;
a one foot rope;
a game with no goal'
a rubber ball with no bounce; and
you're life with no purpose.
We should have divorced long ago.

Retreat

Early summer continues to blossom, but

from my picture window

three dying trees

across the road, waving

good-bye.

Rain and sun together

form puddles in the tiny pockmarks

in the sidewalk like shimmering silver coins.

I smile—thankful that I had known you.

David Ben Foster

Answers

Dependent, controlled, cared about by the will of others,
small minds teasing mine with optimistic rhetoric,
from a Book that they misinterpret;
but I can't soar like the hawk every day,
I need to nest, to ignore my torment, and to consider my
restrictions—
I'm not an eagle.

Spineless, self-serving surrogates of dishonesty
who teach, and then shy away from their own instruction
at the flash of some challenge or revelation,
disquieting as that may seem;
the ancient credos have their limitations,
and so do modern day seers.

Anthrópos

True wisdom,
acquired through suffering,
never superficial; yet
pain, unlike suffering,
flits upward spiriting away
soon to return chiding the afflicted—but
suffering penetrates the spirit.

This carving of the soul
is where wisdom is birthed;
recreating long-held opinions
where life becomes a livable existence
viewed through new eyes.
Wisdom is never discovered
in short lived whirlwinds, like
those taught by false prophets who
stir up powered dust, their
magic.

They are sages of supernatural
buffoonery, dispensing
the mystical, as if one
merely plucked a grape
from the vine of self-serving knowledge.

David Ben Foster

Suffering, wisdom, love, a process toward perfection of the soul.

Betrayal

Betrayal—
intentions gone awry
fidelity compromised,
a self-destructive predicament.
Reason lied.
Penance, never enough;
love stained.
Clothed in humility,
forgiveness remains
the paradox.

David Ben Foster

* CAMILLE

A forlorn gaze...
    dark intriguing eyes
    slender beauty endowed by nature
    unrecognized, rejected in spring
    became the gifted:
    bestowing to the world
    from an injured soul
    sculpture inspired in youthful realism.
Delicate hands
    in the quiet of each contemplation
    movements, liquid in a dim light
    creating timelessness.
Never loved for long
    Joy—momentary lapses
    life was predominantly sadness,
    faithful to the unfaithful,
    in the end alone.
Listening to the rhythm of a pounding surf
    the heavy beat of a weakened heart
    often opened her blue eyes to late mornings;
    days staring in thought.

*Camille Claudel, French sculptor

Can't Write

Rain

the sound of boiling grease...

restless

turning
      stretching

             jerking

on my bed

like a wounded animal

my chest on fire

in the chill of a morning sun.

Hearing a familiar cadence

hollow as my life

    and

fixed upon the course

of a river pushing... pushing.

David Ben Foster

Changeable

If I could ride the wind I would;
to solace far beyond despair
where blossoms sweet as spring and fair
would draw my senses as they should.
My head, always my head, pounding.
Night or day, with family or friends,
I can't escape, it never ends.
Often now a ring resounding
like a phone far-off vibrating,
as I lick my dry thin lips, pursed,
waiting in vain to quench my thirst.
Useless quest. How irritating.
Dreary, this intrusion to earth
by me, where fear and hopelessness
rob me, strip me of blessedness;
shivering, questioning my worth.

Once quickened by the voice of her,
telling tears warm upon her cheeks,
frightened by my torment these weeks,
unsettled in her soul, unsure
if I'd return to love's embrace;
where, as if inspired from heaven,

pour out what should have been given:

the best of me, kissing her face.

David Ben Foster

Dante's Glutton

My wealth well known, drew guests of fame
but sneers from scoundrels born to falter
over excuses, at last to blame men of success, like me.
My brothers often attended these festive feasts, unrestrained,
laughing, drinking, and sumptuously sharing my gluttony.
Intoxicating nights, wearing conceit like a gold chain
moving as a man charmed by a divine, an enigma to myself.
Lavish parties became habitual when I was forty-eight.

Breakfast at noonday brought dirty beggars to my gate
peering with hollow eyes or spanning their reedy bodies
across the entry—some days, disgustingly, dogs licked their wounds.
"This affair was not my doing, surely God knew that!"
I continued indulging despite anger at the unwanted.

Sipping red wine at three or four, I'd pray that death
would swallow them, ridding my estate of these lowborn.
Then on some impulse of good I sent servants to scatter
crumbs before them, like dogs after scraps they snatched the morsels.
I smiled, filled my mouth with wine and mused,
"Perhaps tomorrow I'll do the same. I'm not all bad."

One warm evening dressed in fine silk and purple robe,
the aroma of delicacies inviting my presence, when suddenly
a stabbing pain pierced my chest, stomach sour,
staggering toward a wall, I fell into a thin blackness, silence ...
A wind, deafening, the whoosh of demon flames engulfed,
my parched tongue swelled, lips smacked; I pulled my hair!
Visions, behind closed eyes of a table set: expensive wines
and savory meats—what, never to taste, consume till sore?

What? I squint and rub my burning eyes
and look upward to the right, bewildered—
the beggar made whole. Am I mad? Lazarus the fool
in paradise? I twist side to side in disbelief.

I pray, "Father Abraham hear my unworthy voice,
water, water, a mere drop of it; is this request too large?"
I bow my head again tormented in regions dim,
"Warn my brothers, young hedonists, imbibing life in gulps."

"They have the prophets,"

David Ben Foster

Embitter-ness

Waiting, for something good in a painted cell

listening to my own breath

as small throbbing, pumps in my ankles like

rats licking my socks.

Oh, the holy books instruct

too late, but maybe light welcomes weariness

to lift it off the anxious soul; but

I snatch peace—in tiny gulps, as

sun-heated air warms my scalp

behind my barred window.

Death is not the bite of bitter darkness,

waiting is…

I mull the lie of guilt,

wait for the cell door to squeak open,

listen to dead air.

Faded Flowers

The only witness,

a frenzied figure peering from the shadow.

In an instant

the surprisingly blind rage of jealous possessiveness

slit her throat, then she fell in maddening silence, except for

his exaggerated breathing.

His lover was gone.

Months whisked by like a recurring nightmare.

A jury, above the law, quieted the truth

as another victim perished into mystic quietude:

rationalization,

evidence ignored,

unreasonable doubt that no one heard

as my family, especially my children, shocked by injustice,

lowered their heads to the contrived rendering: *Not guilty*.

New construction—unearthed the knife.

David Ben Foster

Fated

Rulers of their lives

speak of sentimental feelings,

when sticky emotions cling,

like little fuzzy particles of white lint.

Uneventful

these remembrances warm the present;

they return to their rightful place

waiting to be summoned

when the dreaminess ignites

the glow of what was.

Me?

A bloodline curse, fixed within.

Wandering without aim beneath a sun,

cloaked in melancholy,

seeing better in the dark.

Wretched state, mercurial bent;

doomed to blackness in their air;

suffocating

energy sapped

tired.

Incomplete

Days
breezes in the night
Whispering promises for tomorrow
false hopes.
This cool air
faceless
genders feelings of anticipation
wetting my tongue
quenching the thirst
eating the stomach.
Confusion
the brightly burning flame
licking the painful wound.
Lost within, myself the thorn;
pieces of the past
unforgettable.
Come love
mix your tears with mine
cleanse the lies
the panic
        the victim's mind
        of anything.

David Ben Foster

Ghost of a Chance

We are
creating moments that blaze
in frozen images at three a.m.
or at other ungodly hours;
snap-shots of clandestine time we capture and clutch
in our minds, memories we'll embellish tomorrow
when we need them.

You don't know how to walk away;
you're worried about his dangerous temper—
like when you found out about
his indiscretions at work, at the club,
and on business trips.

Beauty in a mess,
change where you should sleep,
to where the very notion of your name
invites the happiest times of my life, and
I vow to be the strength you need to form the words
to break free of him.
Why the hesitation?
Unshackle that irrational bond
for my concentration is fixed on a new vow.

Healed

My eyes conceal, forbid the telling tears.
I'm sure my smile, which often lies, reveals
the dark within—unwarned the fear appears.
This ache, this double-mindedness appeals
to you, your love, your nakedness, that touch
when I succumb, this fool falls down as drugged,
while I arise, yet never me so much
 as you, your soul in mine, entwined, I'm hugged
away at last from senselessness, unrest.
Absurdity laid waste—its death my birth.
You kiss my brow, awakened thoughts caressed.
The hush, our breath as one, unceasing worth;
I never knew this view of you, your grace,
forgiving, healing tears upon your face

David Ben Foster

I Am a Ghost

I am a ghost, quite void of willfulness and hope;
pre-thought possessed the head, but now I grope
to form some notion, as I stir about
as only this soul ought. At last, to pout—
so eager for a more rigorous life;
yet pushed by spirit toward added strife
in spooky ramble of meds, and muse
in night dreams of what I had been—a ruse.

This trick on me, by whomever, is foul,
rancorous—still expected long ago
reduces not, nor softens haunting scowl
when fog settles in on dying ego.
I'm never stoked for any event, they
all simply come and go; reason escapes
me as to why nothing peaks my mind—nay
something: these things in my thoughts: two townscapes
where I had lived, where burdens were gentle
for I didn't write in those carefree days,
nor possessed a passion, nor the mental
gloom tormenting life in curious ways.
I write to prevent insanity, to
keep it at a detached distance—I do.

At some dire time, I'd became a shade

unknown to most, and ever to evade.

A small amount of madness keeps moving

energy in two directions, so this

Gemini stretches up, down, and grooving

to music unheard, yet ever aimless

until I write. At least, terrors at night

have ceased their macabre intrusions with dreams

so horrific—awakened, utter fright

holding me as thought real; the high-pitched screams

filled the air as I fled bed, down the hall,

descending the staircase nothing could forestall

their grip—psychosis near again; nighttime

horrors, not for a spook—a paradigm.

Years do not attach to me at New Years;

I glide bumpily through time; fewer fears.

Less anxiety, more or less musing;

Muse, a liar with a smile, to tease

me to believe in joy; quite amusing

to embrace—a hopelessness haunting squeeze,

like empty trust, or like scrutiny

of fractured light from a Christmas frieze—

a bogus dimension or destiny;

why can't this ghost find some kind of ease?

David Ben Foster

Paintings with light or not, and head tilted
creating emotions—I do not see.
Mental lapses, mislaid words—brain filtered;
then I shout in my head, after I hear her plea,
"You make no damn sense." The bloody left eye
flutters uncontrolled—bad night—no ally.

There ensues to mind—there is no defense.
I refuse the fate of Berryman and
Plath—not in judgment nor any pretense
except when I spiral down; no will; grand
coercion; powerless; helpless to know;
mind in a frenzy, like a spayed cat; shove,
pull; Muse like an abusive wife; although,
unyielding prodding, laughing at love
and Zoloft, knowing that neither perform—
although both should; so a ghost belongs in
an undercroft; he knows how to conform;
where his secrets have life; he therein
bothers no one, no meds, values, or barb;
imbalanced stomach ache needs no bicarb.
Esophageal spasm, where flux
locks and scorches like fire; can't nourish;
water is dammed; naught passes the crux—
hot meal goes to waste; I stare at the dish,
then walk away in pain. Soon the flabby

tummy begs its return when the bind is

free, but appetite has passed; I'm crabby,

tired, and I don't dare approach the misses.

I am aloof, moody, and quite myself;

lost in a daze, every day—the ghost;

for this is the main condition itself;

the one despised, ever loathed the most.

The guinea pig just ended a central

sleep apnea test—painful, hose and all.

Night ended; cleaned up the mask; longing for

flight is unquenchable; the transmitters—

off—on the creative side of the brain, for

it prickles the skin, and causes jitters;

should back off in writing more verse, or

pull a blanket past the chin, blink an eye

at the moon peeping through the glass in the door;

close both eyes; attempt to sleep; apply

the CPAP; turn it on; begins to trap

my head—tightly with an elastic strap.

Rubber made for inside the nose—push, snap.

Annoyance, discomfort, distress—what crap.

Who knows what this contraption aids—never

heals. Repetitive routine forever.

There is no ambiguity in that mood,

David Ben Foster

skin works in harmony like fraternal twins:

twitch and itch. There is no reason to brood;

I can't attain, nor can she, no one wins.

Flash: obstructive sleep apnea is now

me: mysterious of all sounds: hummm,

lying motionless, like a statue; wow,

all night: hummm, hummm, hummm.

There is no balm for aggravated nights;

vigor unchanged; this apparition

that I am, lost continuously, fights

for cognition, for reason, volition.

Learned to Surrender

Whoever she is, she's only for the short run, a season, never a year.
Yet, she is always worth my meager time.
We ran and laughed as waves beckoned us to the sea;
with the same sort of attraction; she teases me with
gestures of desire with her arms outstretched,
head tilted, seductive smile; I wondered how long
before she too ends our hyphenated romance, a relationship
not unlike the bond or shackle of past lovers.
You're not unlovable, she said waving goodbye; but
the next day, a tight skirt that matched her dark, smooth leathery skin
said hello to me at the golf course.

David Ben Foster

Petty Kings

In phantasms of authority

striving for more

she is unable to relinquish;

after all, she gave power to him

at the altar;

beaming father and father-in-law

querying mothers

smiling priest

in a church full of nodding souls

and their banality of male domination

should blow in holy dust.

The melody sung by early women

muted by screaming small men;

her optimism

other women.

Me?

I dare not expect to understand
something impossible to fathom;
heart and mind collide in a vacuum
where soaring in joy
and driven downward
in the same swirl of life
is my existence.
Perverse
profane
commonplace reality.

David Ben Foster

Performing

I get a stir each time you touch me,
then remember its not me you're thoughts embrace
it's the last guy
that held you
or one of them
who made your eyes appear heavenly
that kept your appetite in check
prevented sleep from your long night
of texting—several of them.
Hurting me, like some unfaithful actress
was not your intention
as you reach out for a better life
while I will be left with
other disloyal
injured admirers.

I had found an empty spot
in a young heart:
I knew better—
jealousy examines all that you do;
suspicion catches every eye
that undresses you;
anger fumes beneath my skin

igniting ill temper.

You elicit tenderness

that will not calm the outburst

you're dragged into so often.

When you say let's give it a rest

you are waiting for my goodbye.

No way

free yourself.

A familiar blue funk

will cover me

like a grey winter day,

but surviving is what I do best.

David Ben Foster

Let Me Be Brave

Beneath my feet

the marching of millions

with determined principle

to reclaim past guarantees.

Indignation at the silent discontent,

whose own blood will stain their hands

when a revolution to preserve

Jeffersonian models breaks down

like walls that crumble under excessive weight;

for when will the silence break

forth? Perhaps the muteness will prevail.

Perception

It's not as though a Potter's Field, I seek;
it's just reprieve from the anguish I cause
my love, ever strong, yet so ever meek.
I've challenged life persistently because
it's more beneficial to try, than not;
she has reminded repeatedly with those
green eyes—her demand may seem like a lot,
as a cluster of maxims stress repose.
I feel the cold, hear the wind pushing it
against the windows in white clear gusts, knowing
she sleeps—at rest from me, an unfit
friend, but her tenderness prevents showing
my grey color; she puts a better face
on me, and refutes my gloomy embrace.

David Ben Foster

Deceptions

From screaming propagandas
so small, but enlarge in less than three generations
and stifle reasonable thinking.

The great war of stalemate,
the world war of unconditional demands,
and all conflicts,
will each pale like a vanishing horse
in light of new irrational conjecture,
just as new foes find succor in the arms
of Washington elite.
American optimism is in glowing ashes
waiting for a new current candor
to fan it into flames,
moving beyond the semblance of integrity—
mere acknowledgement of truth is not adherence.

The revolutionary acquisition
of founding fathers and
their ingenious constitutional rights
are not dead speculations in many minds;
money, that old golden temptation
pays political prostitutes
who whimper about

"for the good of all,"

"reinterpretation of Constitutional precepts

that are theory," or more precise, "fluid premises," and

these snobby officials rely on allies:

robed lawyers on the Supreme Court.

Their inglorious retreat,

with sounds of sniveling,

is treachery, for they are

the enemies living in the greatest

Republic ever—new enemies arriving daily.

I hear the thunder.

David Ben Foster

Miscommunication

His love, enough for now, though

impassioned earlier in the relationship;

yet, her deception widened more than love—

late night meetings, phone calls, or

if home, television.

As he tried to improve, her affection waned

like a double-minded school girl,

unable to remain with one suitor.

In time, insecurity plagued his inattentiveness

with slight rejections of her—

paranoia turned to fear.

He turned his head for a peck on the cheek,

felt her hand just as cold,

said goodbye from the doorway,

and found late work to do

in his study.

One night, as contempt deprived his sleep,

she never came home.

Nothing New

I stooped to watch the slush and rush

of dirty water

in an open ended drain

hurrying into the small forest

behind the old stone smoke house

on Father's fifty-four acres.

Rain pelted my cap

as I remembered how large

that little moving stream looked

when I had worn a small Indians ball cap

thirty years before as smoke rose

from the curing process that I had hated.

I had nothing more to detest—

there was nothing more to prove;

his legal will brought me home.

The dilapidated place—mine.

The warm July rain

suddenly decided to give the small stream a break;

I stood and wiped my hands on a rag

I had used earlier, I noticed a small scratch

on each hand, and

stretched out my fingers to check for more—

David Ben Foster

to my sullen surprise, I had his hands.

My son threw a stone into the water.

What?

It is quite doubtful that the mere act of sex
done tastefully
is an act of love,
nor can passion be separated from art.
A person dieing of thirst doesn't sip;
a painter cannot produce a pastoral scene
without dimensions.
Latitude is not void of restrictions, and
abandon remains an icon of the intellect,
not merely a human effort of egotism;
nevertheless, each morning I hear the refrain,
"I love her love of me."

David Ben Foster

Severe

The naughty and nice view life in shaded ways—
as darlings cured or devils of the cursed,
sailing or wobbling in short or long days;
their melodies, never ever rehearsed,
although extremes, and neither find an end.
Middle ground is academic fodder, bland
and of no value to the psyche, nor a friend
to any human endeavor; understand
this: gods, friendless spirits themselves, myself
an authority, become absorbed, blind
in their ambition, pull tight the cord, each self
stretched like a noose until there is no mind.
When shadows overcome, eternity's
fingers will close eyes, darken dignities.

Repetition

I fear, I fail in love more than succeed;
and not as a nuance of wrong, some sense
of ill to haunt your mind, cause it to bleed
the joyfulness or happiness from whence
our love had been born—against the odds;
 for our romance, a stepping stone to find
a truer love determined by the gods
who dine on my pain, who divine in kind
misfortune to such lovers—jaded souls,
sneering, alluring new lovers to draw near
to their invented temptations for failed goals;
and so my heart succumbs to lust and fear.
The enticement intensifies, and then,
with no fault of yours, I'll be gone again.

David Ben Foster

Not Mine

Teasing waves of brunette as you walk

into the next room;

green Irish eyes that catch mine

on the elevator; and

full sculptured lips that speak, smile,

and broaden into laughter at lunch with your friends.

Why is my life defined by you?

I'm still chasing

dodging thoughts of loss

wishing more than I should

from my cocoon, a corner office.

At night, when I walk to my apartment

shadows pull at my jacket, the way you used to do,

and yet, all my problems would puddle

at my feet, if you were mine.

When, I

When doing what I dislike

guilt oozes from my pores

like liquid that is sticky and clear;

it suffocates thinking, closing my throat

as my lips become dry.

Disappointment, disgust, and anger,

seem unable to resolve even unintentional failings

that life had intended for me

long before I had been birthed.

This incessant dripping on my head from some heavenly brush

painting my life in hideous blotches is itself unforgiving.

When I dwell on these black spots inside,

I need a dark room or even a closed closet

to find a moment of reprieve

David Ben Foster

New Year's Eve

Others dream, scheme on New Years Eve:

resolutions of reform,

improvements they cannot believe.

Reaching for the newness of the night:

Desire—the cup,

Coveting—the potion,

Calculating—the toast, the hope

of what could be.

Here we are, a moment ahead.

Knowing—

love leads as lovers trust

plans encompass the gifts we are

surpassing the semblance most common.

Love—the elixir

Sharing—the chalice

Conviction—the joy of all we're becoming—

for now.

Then, You

My soul, hidden from others,

replete with bitter loss.

Uncertain of myself, unsure of you.

Seductive smiles, inviting eyes

turned my head, not heart.

Shallow gestures from

hollow souls who weep, often before the dawn,

in vacuums life created.

Then, you, fresh as truth;

willingly, compellingly I bid you,

placing the key to me

into your waiting mind.

Taking my warm hand into yours

we unlocked my soul.

David Ben Foster

Regret

Return—

my faded self

needs your gentle strokes,

brushing color into our affection.

Restore—

communion betrayed,

mingled wine, misplaced vows.

Renew—

unplanned moments

which engulfed our passions

anywhere in warm rain

anytime love charged our

ardent lust to be one.

Tilted

Depression
  unrelenting voice
  inescapable seducement
  with promises of sweet solitude;
  unforgivable lies
In and out
  of a cold world
  warmed by anger within
  hearing murmurs in turbulence,
  like rushing wind near the ocean,
  battered to the bone
  along a corridor, crudely savage
  even the green swampy gulf
  pales in intensity.

David Ben Foster

Traveler

Like a wayward ship

sailing on wide and narrow

waterways

never dropping anchor

long enough to make friends—

why burden dear souls

with lies of great adventure

leaving them to dream,

to imagine something unreal.

Leaving them as they were,

sailing off to black nights

so ebony that it crawls on my skin...

Alone

at the mercy of Nature,

that alluring beauty

who can viciously turn like a

fire from hell,

not to consume

to leave me naked, but

to will my return,

perhaps the final scene.

Medication

Mirroring the reasons

for depressions

arguments within

not blues, those prickly inconveniences

an optimist can scratch away;

I

scorched by brightness of what could be;

as brittle and frail as onion skin;

stuck in what is;

an annoyance to myself.

David Ben Foster

The Black Is Back

The black is back

the sweat inside

burning, burning,

fear and fire

hopelessness in my disease

as the smoke of anger chokes,

and anxiousness evokes the worst,

controlling me.

Not my will, but its.

Vibrations of life un-tuned.

My very being unfits

the space I take...

the world moves over.

NAM 1968

Living the nightmare

briefly warned about in training.

Deserting the rumor of wrong

obeying the heart of duty

placed in a culture

foreign,

except the pain, death, and

the occasional smile of gratitude

from tired faces remembered

from another war.

I brought an M-16, the will to survive,

and a mere pocket full of hope

in the name of freedom

to stand ground I'd never own.

Soon the worst of life, in the prime of life,

consumed my consciousness.

Sweat and fear, evidence of bravery,

smelling the heat

in tension which smothered,

I remembered home,

never believing any of them

would forget me.

David Ben Foster

Pitch Blue

On an invisible line of the honored
The colors wave in parallel
on a perpendicular shaft of grey
overlooking human misery; misery
masked by duty
as red runs in puddles.

Star-crossed

I spoke with distant stars;

played in moving shadows of dark trees

as a half-moon blew breezes

through mid-night skies.

My love for you, in vain but true

came to mind

as warm air lightly kissed my face,

for I had ever believed that you were enough,

but you slept the sleep

of those who falter,

unsure, unaware that love is never safety.

I could never embrace

your dreamlessness,

the stranger you were, you are.

The quiet hush of the heavens

invited me again

to listen to the assurance of the stars,

promising tomorrow.

David Ben Foster

Miasma

I never with intention bruised your heart;
that tender gift of you, never in view
when ugly fears so deep and grave ensue.
This injury to you, to me—a mark,
a blot, on worthy devotion, defiles
the joy, the happiness behind your eyes.
Dispirited, the gloom pervades with lies,
and in this weariness, I see your smiles.
Beguiled, then snatched and pulled into the mist
until I'm there, abandoned in the rift,
a gulf so gray and great, I merely drift
as though I've known no other state, and missed
by not a soul, and damned to ever die
while you remain impassioned to this lie.

Mirage

I was you
thinking that I was the same to you.
Wanting only a better life, but
now remembering your nodding affirmations that built walls.

Your smile—the lure,
to hold on to what
I thought was *us*.
The lie—your heart reserved
for itself, a bottomless pool
where only your reflection on the surface
shocked me.
Not narcissistic—needy,
unable to see me,
blinded by the glare of self.

David Ben Foster

Mistress

Nights come upon me like taunting evils,
goading my soul, boastfully as it wills.
Deep is the dark of the hours before me;
my submissive spirit waits anxiously
for the first hint of day, which dissipates;
the obscurity of night my soul hates.
Soft shadows which embrace and inflame
entangle our bodies, you breathe my name.
Be my gentle zephyr; pull me to your breast,
let me find release, ever sweet caress.

Intention

I never with design would bruise your heart;
the precious gift of you is not in view
when ugly fear in me projects askew.
The injury that came my way once part

of me, the four year old, could not escape
from women in erotic pose in sleek
and silky nylon hose; they'd pinch my cheek,
removed our clothes, and fear soon scarred inscape.*

Beguiled by you, I prayed the gloom would fade
like nightmares do as days ensue, as life
crowds in; but, must I drift in years, sweet wife,
in gloom, distrust, and jade? Should it pervade

to thieve from us what's not your fault? Don't leave.
I'm damned again if you do— please believe.

---

*a person's inner nature

David Ben Foster

Last Cigarette

Lake Erie's cold in December

I'd been told, can't remember by whom.

Someone said, of all her dead

that going down was beautiful—by whom?

I suck a drag, blow blue swirls into the cold

and wonder if anyone lived to tell a survivor's tail.

No matter...

I pull at the oars, pull, pull—far enough;

I envision: music soft, from far off, as lazy thoughts awake

a real crazy trip to take to a land so beautiful.

Floating, sinking, swept away to another day

where stresses cease in a kinda peace

I hope, then

button up my coat...

Contemplations

What seems acceptable often falls short—
like dribble when drunk, or a curious drool
staring at a 357 magnum
cradled in my arms
like a newborn.
Life is like drifting—
a lift or swoon of emotion
where happiness blinks or
flutters, yet always fleeting;
like a cancer that wanes
but returns to steal hope.
The inescapable, incessant crawling within;
trapped in a mirror, saddened behind the glass
as self-help trickles into my shoes, and
ancient lies beat a foreign sound.

David Ben Foster

Wide Nights

Narrow days, but wide nights

beat in a twenty-four/seven rhythm—

how manic, wants to be heard,

whispering to me now, without a voice;

and my shadow rests often fixed

against a plain painted wall in a cell,

my bedroom, lighted by a single bulb at

bedside, yet my eyes feel too large, itch for sleep.

The nightly fixation, exaggeration, and debilitation as

the incessant sounds, "one—two— one—two"

as the small knick-knack clock ticks—

a mahogany gift that one day, I hope to re-gift.

Then there is a kind of syncopation, the "blep—belp—blep"

from a faucet until I'm forced to do something

about these vociferous and un-welcomed vocals

with new overhead light as I read or write

and wait for day

with thirty-second-nods every couple of hours.

I work every thin day—not without migraines.

Boxed in a room of words—mine;

walls move and dark shadows stick

as uneven glaring sunlight seems to move the drapes.

The Sense of It

Night freezes like black ice

trapping me beneath it

stamping unspeakable images behind

my staring, eyes wide open.

Why do I often see what is not there?

No attempt is made to rescue me, so

I sense—leave it alone.

Be a troop of one, fighting within,

lost, looking through the glass-like veneer

fixed above me. Who could define this

unpleasantness; this troublesome state of being?

David Ben Foster

Birthmark

When rest ignores my weariness at night
though I implore its mercy as a fool.
I oft resent what men have deemed as right
and shrug my heavy shoulders at their drool.
When death invites with deep deceptive tones,
and lingers with its question, as a friend,
I'm not as apt to send him off in groans,
he's right, "We'll pay for sins we cannot mend."
And cynicism colors vast domain
his callousness, in miasma, gives birth;
who slinks about in stink, and knows my name,
in unconcern, in loathsomeness on earth;
so fixed is the stain, like a facial birthmark,
will and hope, lie still within profound dark.

Impasse

I slowly drift into a sullen mood
and unexpectedly, comes the change.
At brief impulsive times you'd flee my brood,
and yet, you know inside that life is strange;
but baby, keep in mind, you're not to blame.
So twisted in a common view of man
where feelings of suspicion often maim,
as they create dislike, I never plan;
there is no way discerning black or white
as though to shun a choice between the two
and no one asks about this bitter plight
it's indecision that stirs this breath of anger too.
Morality, mere philosophical
concession that blends with the comical.

David Ben Foster

Wedged

Pacing…pacing like a caged panther

dark and moody with senses quick, intense

with every glance, a study in the sick pretense

of life as the heart of me lifts my snug t-shirt with

little flutters I feel in my wrists;

midnight and an unexpected fever

is welcomed bringing a sort of rest, alien as that is;

wait—I can't sleep

caught between the moon and day

circling the room,

now from room to room with

strides not unlike an animal,

listening for someone to care.

Less of Me

Anticipating while reclining in vain with a migraine

imagining a better day, one that is five years past,

Turning from one side to the other, only

to stare at grey walls, hearing my own sighing

in the ambiguity of how I arrived at this juncture.

Less than a man; she no less of herself—more of

friend, as she, a partner to herself.

Beauty still draws me to her dead passion,

to the girlish smile, to the tender heart of a mother.

Indeed, disappointed expectations of couched thoughts—

a man not a man

a lover nowhere around; punished for

mistakes unwittingly made, and

only heard about the blunders years

later when I questioned the embarrassments,

that had brought such dreadful penalties,

I had not seen such before.

I waken to the unending, reproving condition—

alone.

David Ben Foster

Inevitably

To love, void of sacrifice, is self-centered, for
investments involve risk, like when I left my wife
for you; when the money was good; when laughing,
often, you were like the school girl you are; and
nothing was limitless;
until I was stifled, put under your direction, and my own
writing began to mock me.
Suppression, in the form of passive aggression,
pushed you further until the guest bedroom wasn't far
enough, and pleasantries disappeared, and even the days
seemed happier when night arrived.

Oneness

I was you—thinking that you were me—
making life better, but
affirmations built insurmountable walls
on collapsing foundations;
Your smile—the lure
to snare the hope within,
turning my eyes only to you.

The lie—a heart that could not love,
a bottomless pool of self, where only
reflections surfaced—not you.

Not narcissistic—needy
unable to see me
callously turning around
in the glare of self-significance.

David Ben Foster

Platonic Love

I alone warm my bed
with either one;
home makes no sense, but
elsewhere is the same.
Bound in the middle,
neither perfect;
alone with either
as reality spoils truth.
My god, surviving meds, marriage, and
the non-sexual love who yet claims fidelity.
From my dark bedroom, noise—soft, like
the hoo hoo of an old owl
alone on a branch, or in the empty barn.
I am the unhealable wound to both
who have fear of some future;
unattainable love at home, untouched love with the other.
Never the object of ridicule; never the point of a joke;
only the brunt of angry words—damn consternation.
Caught in a platonic shadow;
living the lie.
Conformity does not fit, but
fallacies exist for me.
Weary, still anxious until

a warm morning sun

closes my eyes in a peaceful moment,

for I know that neither bed is possible.

David Ben Foster

Last Words

All Libertarians want—left alone;

earth-based faith—New Age;

No Islam—safeguarding culture—Japan.

Maximum speed in 1915—10.

Cognitive indifference—deliberate.

Prelate power—shrewd.

War in the mind—psychosis.

Wide eyed expectation—faith.

Less often used verb—love.

Trichotomy—man.

Sexually transmitted—life

The art of medicine—practice.

Smack-talk—friendly fire.

Snapchat—millennials.

Most active at night—brain.

No one above the law—yeah.

Ranks in military—pecking order.

Stagnant innovation—contentment.

Do nothing about evil—decay.

Autobiography—filter.

Tributary through human complexities—poet.

Death of your child—haunting.

American Party—George Washington

Biology and creativity—music.

Never extremism—virtue.

Embody an idea—best expression.

Love of money—slavery.

Word to the wise—sufficient.

Complex puzzle—life.

Fatal stumbling—egotism.

A principal mistake—surrendering.

David Ben Foster

Happy that you met me…

When morning windows, with an orange glow,

opened my eyes, I sensed

that days ahead would be improved.

My response was to resolve

to challenge distress

for love was to dispel discontent;

loves had been sought that were like

shooting stars.

Others like the tide rolling in—gone in the morning.

I knew when you gave me

a half smile, then started to say something;

but walked away.

Tender had been your embrace;

there were no promises;

shallow quick breathes;

no completeness—you couldn't help it.

I will never say your name again;

I'd rather have a shooting star;

but there's a flash of happiness when

I think of how we met.

Island Adjustment

Her playhouse burned—now

beneath ascending smoke;

she, alone in change.

Change, the chance

for liberation from the crowded

life;

lift up your spirit

release each breathe anew

for the grey New York streets

live in anxiety no more.

Each borough has options

with new visions.

Dark grey ash stirs

in puffs around her thongs.

Days turn to ten, while she sits

at a bus station; light rain

forms odd pockets of water in dry

colorful leaves.

She thinks back to a bench

in the park, thoughts of inadequateness

Can I write in another city?

She grabbed her packed bag;

David Ben Foster

entered the bus; sat back

with closed eyes.

She squinted open her eyes to a shrinking skyline;

the moon was hiding.

Months of small jobs,

Traveling, driven by pain,

homesick, haunted by loss,

always looking back.

"I trust the uncertainty of New York.

Although I had slept restlessly

Most of the nights away, I had been

awakened by familiar music

that brought an unexpected smile.

Manhattan had broken my heart,

but I gathered my things up, and

bought bus fare for home;

summer brings a million new beginnings

in my island city."

Interludes

With warm illusions I watch

the moon lift slowly to

heavens colored in blues.

Suddenly, remembered—her light borrowed;

like air I breathe.

Memories wane,

reality changes,

for a moment, I'm free.

David Ben Foster

Wild Flower

I remember minutes from this quiet day as I lay

my head on the pillow,

and smile…

Soft breezes gently rustled branches

in the summer heat;

a butterfly jerked though a soundless midafternoon,

and a wild flower reminded me of you;

I know not how long thoughts brushed against memories

of you, but soon they awakened me

to night terrors.

www.ingramcontent.com/pod-product-compliance
Lightning Source LLC
Chambersburg PA
CBHW060212050426
42446CB00013B/3057